# Del Monte Quality
## Quick & Easy Recipes

Publications International, Ltd.

This edition published by Publications International, Ltd., 7373 N. Cicero Ave.,
Lincolnwood, IL 60646.

All recipes developed and tested in the Del Monte Kitchens.

Photography on pages 11, 13, 19, 23, 25, 27, 29, 39, 43, 47, 55, 59, 61, 69, 71, 73,
and 77 by Burke/Triolo Productions, Culver City, CA.

**Pictured on the front cover:** Garden Primavera Pasta *(page 52).*
**Pictured on the back cover** *(clockwise from top left):* Tomato Chicken Gumbo
*(page 18);* Sweet and Spicy Chicken Stir-Fry *(page 58);* Pear-Ginger Sorbet, Simple
Peach Sorbet and Piña Colada Sorbet *(page 84).*

ISBN: 0-7853-1630-2

Manufactured in U.S.A.

8    7    6    5    4    3    2    1

**Preparation and Cooking Times**: The preparation times are based on the
approximate amount of time required to assemble the recipe before cooking, baking,
chilling or serving. These times include preparation steps such as measuring,
chopping and mixing. The fact that some preparations and cooking can be done
simultaneously is taken into account and a total Prep & Cook Time is given.
Preparation of optional ingredients and serving suggestions is not included.

**Microwave Cooking:** Microwave ovens vary in wattage. The microwave cooking
times given in this publication are approximate. Use the cooking times as guidelines
and check for doneness before adding more time. Consult the manufacturer's
instructions for suitable microwave-safe cooking dishes.

# The Del Monte Difference

**The Del Monte name goes back more than 100 years to when the Oakland Preserving Company named their premium quality canned goods Del Monte, "from the mountain." Today, consumers know the Del Monte brand stands for premium quality, just as it did 100 years ago. When you buy Del Monte, you're buying the best.**

• The high heat used in the canning process preserves the food just like home canning does, so we never need to add preservatives.

• At Del Monte, we can most of our fruits and vegetables within 24 hours of harvesting, when flavor and nutrients are at their peaks.

• Del Monte canned fruits, vegetables and tomatoes are on hand and affordable year-round, when seasonal produce may be unavailable.

• Fruits, vegetables and tomatoes packed under our label meet strict quality standards.

• Our cans are recyclable steel— they're made with 30% recycled steel, the maximum amount that could be used.

• More than 20 years ago, Del Monte was the first company to use voluntary nutritional labeling and was one of the first to comply with the latest nutritional labeling regulations.

• Our fruits, vegetables and tomatoes add variety and a balance of nutrients to your diet. These convenient products make it easy to eat your "5-A-Day". Eating 5 or more servings of fruit and vegetables daily is recommended by the National Cancer Institute, the U.S. Department of Health and Human Services, the U.S. Department of Agriculture and the National Academy of Sciences.

• At Del Monte, we are in tune with today's lifestyles and consumer trends, so we offer a line of products that gives you, the consumer, a choice. Our tomatoes are precut and preseasoned, ready to make quick sauces, soups and entrées. Our tomato and vegetable products come in regular or no-salt-added varieties. Our fruits are packed in heavy or light syrup, or in 100% natural juice. We make single serving SNACK CUPS® products that are convenient, ready-to-eat and delicious— and they don't need refrigeration.

# Hearty Soups & Stews

## TOMATO FRENCH ONION SOUP

4 medium onions, chopped
2 tablespoons butter or margarine
1 can (14½ ounces) DEL MONTE® Italian Recipe Stewed
   Tomatoes
1 can (10½ ounces) condensed beef consommé
¼ cup dry sherry
4 French bread slices, toasted
1½ cups (6 ounces) shredded Swiss cheese
¼ cup (1 ounce) grated Parmesan cheese

**1.** In large saucepan, cook onions in butter about 10 minutes. Drain
tomatoes, reserving liquid. Chop tomatoes. Add tomatoes, reserved liquid,
2 cups water, consommé and sherry to saucepan. Bring to boil, skimming
off foam.

**2.** Reduce heat to medium-low; simmer 10 minutes. Place soup in four
broilerproof bowls; top with bread and cheeses. Broil until cheese is melted
and golden.

*4 servings*

**Prep & Cook Time:** 35 minutes

**Helpful Hint:** If broilerproof bowls are not available, place soup in
ovenproof bowls and bake at 350°F, 10 minutes.

# RAVIOLI SOUP

nces) fresh or frozen cheese ravioli or

¾ pound hot Italian sausage, crumbled
1 can (14½ ounces) DEL MONTE® Italian Recipe Stewed
    Tomatoes
1 can (14 ounces) beef broth
1 can (14½ ounces) DEL MONTE Italian Green Beans,
    drained
2 green onions, sliced

**1.** Cook pasta according to package directions; drain.

**2.** Meanwhile, cook sausage in 5-quart pot over medium-high heat until no longer pink; drain. Add tomatoes, broth and 1¾ cups water; bring to boil.

**3.** Reduce heat to low; stir in pasta, green beans and green onions. Simmer until heated through. Season with pepper and sprinkle with grated Parmesan cheese, if desired.                    *4 servings*

**Prep & Cook Time:** 15 minutes

Ravioli Soup

# FISHERMAN'S SOUP

⅛ teaspoon dried thyme, crushed
½ pound halibut or other firm white fish
2 tablespoons vegetable oil
1 medium onion, chopped
1 clove garlic, crushed
3 tablespoons all-purpose flour
2 cans (14 ounces *each*) low-salt chicken broth
1 can (15¼ ounces) DEL MONTE® Whole Kernel Golden
    Sweet Corn, No Salt Added, undrained
1 can (14½ ounces) DEL MONTE Whole New Potatoes,
    drained and chopped

**1.** Sprinkle thyme over both sides of fish. In large saucepan, cook fish in 1 tablespoon hot oil over medium-high heat until fish flakes easily when tested with a fork. Remove fish from saucepan; set aside.

**2.** Heat remaining 1 tablespoon oil in same saucepan over medium heat. Add onion and garlic; cook until onion is tender. Stir in flour; cook 1 minute. Stir in broth; cook until thickened, stirring occasionally. Stir in corn and potatoes.

**3.** Discard skin and bones from fish; cut fish into bite-sized pieces.

**4.** Just before serving, add fish to soup; heat through. Stir in chopped parsley or sliced green onions, if desired.                                    *4 to 6 servings*

**Prep Time:** 5 minutes
**Cook Time:** 12 minutes

**Fisherman's Soup**

# SPICY QUICK AND EASY CHILI

1 pound ground beef
1 large clove garlic, minced
1 can (15¼ ounces) DEL MONTE® Whole Kernel Golden
    Sweet Corn, drained
1 can (16 ounces) kidney beans, drained
1½ cups DEL MONTE Picante or Traditional Salsa, Mild,
    Medium or Hot
1 can (4 ounces) diced green chiles, undrained

**1.** In large saucepan, brown meat with garlic; drain.

**2.** Add remaining ingredients. Simmer, uncovered, 10 minutes, stirring occasionally. Sprinkle with chopped green onions, if desired.    *4 servings*

**Prep & Cook Time:** 15 minutes

# CREAMY ASPARAGUS POTATO SOUP

1 can (15 ounces) DEL MONTE® Asparagus Spears, drained
1 can (14½ ounces) DEL MONTE New Potatoes, drained
½ teaspoon dried thyme, crushed
⅛ teaspoon garlic powder
1 can (14 ounces) chicken broth
1 cup milk or half & half

**1.** Place asparagus, potatoes, thyme and garlic powder in food processor or blender (in batches, if needed); process until smooth.

**2.** Pour into medium saucepan; add broth. Bring to boil. Stir in milk; heat through. *(Do not boil.)* Season with salt and pepper to taste, if desired. Serve hot or cold. Thin with additional milk or water, if desired.

    *4 servings*

**Prep Time:** 5 minutes
**Cook Time:** 5 minutes

**Spicy Quick and Easy Chili**

# CAJUN CHILI

6 ounces spicy sausage links, sliced
4 boneless chicken thighs, skinned and cut into cubes
1 medium onion, chopped
⅛ teaspoon cayenne pepper
1 can (15 ounces) black-eyed peas or kidney beans, drained
1 can (14½ ounces) DEL MONTE® FRESH CUT™ Diced
    Tomatoes with Garlic & Onion, undrained
1 medium green bell pepper, chopped

**1.** In large skillet, lightly brown sausage over medium-high heat. Add chicken, onion and cayenne pepper; cook until browned. Drain.

**2.** Stir in remaining ingredients. Cook 5 minutes, stirring occasionally.

*4 servings*

**Prep & Cook Time:** 20 minutes

# SOUTHERN BBQ CHILI

½ pound lean ground beef
1 medium onion, chopped
1 clove garlic, minced
1½ cups DEL MONTE® Picante or Traditional Salsa, Mild
1 can (15 ounces) barbecue-style beans
1 can (15 ounces) black beans, drained
1 can (8¾ ounces) or 1 cup kidney beans, drained

**1.** In large saucepan, brown meat with onion and garlic; drain.

**2.** Add salsa and beans. Cover and simmer 15 minutes or until heated through. Top with sour cream and sliced green onions, if desired.

*6 servings*

**Prep Time:** 5 minutes
**Cook Time:** 20 minutes

**Cajun Chili**

# TOMATO CHICKEN GUMBO

6 chicken thighs
½ pound hot sausage links or Polish sausage, sliced
1 can (14 ounces) chicken broth
½ cup uncooked long-grain white rice
1 can (26½ ounces) DEL MONTE® Traditional or Chunky
    Garlic and Herb Spaghetti Sauce
1 can (11 ounces) DEL MONTE SUMMER CRISP™ Corn,
    drained
1 medium green bell pepper, diced

**1.** Preheat oven to 400°F. In large shallow baking pan, place chicken and sausage. Bake 35 minutes or until chicken is no longer pink in center. Cool slightly.

**2.** Remove skin from chicken; cut meat into cubes. Cut sausage into slices ½ inch thick.

**3.** In 6-quart pot, bring broth and 3 cups water to boil. Add chicken, sausage and rice. Cover; cook over medium heat 15 minutes.

**4.** Stir in remaining ingredients; bring to boil. Cover; cook 5 minutes or until rice is tender.                                    *4 servings*

**Prep & Cook Time:** 1 hour

**Tip:** Add additional water or broth for a thinner gumbo. For spicier gumbo, serve with hot red pepper sauce.

**Tomato Chicken Gumbo**

# FRENCH BEEF STEW

1½ pounds stew beef, cut into 1-inch cubes
¼ cup all-purpose flour
2 tablespoons vegetable oil
2 cans (14½ ounces *each*) DEL MONTE® Original Recipe
   Stewed Tomatoes
1 can (14 ounces) beef broth
4 medium carrots, peeled and cut into 1-inch chunks
2 medium potatoes, peeled and cut into 1-inch chunks
¾ teaspoon dried thyme, crushed
2 tablespoons Dijon mustard (optional)

**1.** Combine meat and flour in large plastic food storage bag; toss to coat evenly.

**2.** In 6-quart saucepan, brown meat in hot oil. Season with salt and pepper, if desired.

**3.** Add all remaining ingredients except mustard. Bring to boil; reduce heat to medium-low. Cover; simmer 1 hour or until beef is tender.

**4.** Blend in mustard. Garnish and serve with warm crusty French bread, if desired.

*6 to 8 servings*

**Prep Time:** 10 minutes
**Cook Time:** 1 hour

French Beef Stew

**Del Monte** Quality

# Satisfying Sides & Salads

## TARRAGON TUNA PASTA SALAD

½ cup mayonnaise
½ teaspoon dried tarragon or thyme, crushed
3 cups chilled cooked mostaccioli or elbow macaroni
2 stalks celery, sliced
1 can (6⅛ ounces) solid white tuna in water, drained and
    broken into bite-sized pieces
1 can (14½ ounces) DEL MONTE® Peas and Carrots,
    drained

**1.** In large bowl, combine mayonnaise and tarragon. Add pasta, celery and tuna. Gently stir in peas and carrots.

**2.** Cover serving plates with lettuce, if desired. Top with salad. Garnish, if desired.                                                                                    *4 servings*

**Prep Time:** 8 minutes

**Healthy Hint:** Use light mayonnaise instead of regular mayonnaise.

# MANDARIN CHICKEN SALAD

1 can (15½ ounces) DEL MONTE® Pineapple Chunks In
    Heavy Syrup, undrained
3 tablespoons vegetable oil
3 tablespoons cider vinegar
1 tablespoon soy sauce
4 cups shredded cabbage or iceberg lettuce
1 can (14½ ounces) DEL MONTE FRESH CUT™ Diced
    Tomatoes, drained
2 cups cubed cooked chicken
⅓ cup packed cilantro, chopped, *or* ½ cup sliced green
    onions

**1.** Drain pineapple, reserving ¼ cup syrup. In small bowl, combine reserved syrup, oil, vinegar and soy sauce; stir briskly with fork.

**2.** In large bowl, toss cabbage with pineapple, tomatoes, chicken and cilantro. Add dressing as desired; gently toss.

**3.** Sprinkle with crumbled dry noodles (from Oriental noodle soup mix), toasted slivered almonds or toasted sesame seeds, if desired.     *4 servings*

**Prep Time:** 15 minutes

# DILLED CARROT SALAD

¼ teaspoon dill weed
1 can (8¼ ounces) DEL MONTE® Sliced Carrots, drained
5 cups torn romaine lettuce
    Dijon dressing

**1.** In large bowl, sprinkle dill over carrots.

**2.** Add lettuce; toss with dressing.     *4 servings*

**Prep Time:** 5 minutes

**Mandarin Chicken Salad**

# CAESAR SHRIMP PASTA SALAD

1 can (14½ ounces) DEL MONTE® FRESH CUT™ Diced
   Tomatoes with Garlic & Onion, undrained
1 pound cooked tiny shrimp
6 cups cooked corkscrew pasta
1 small cucumber, diced
1 cup Caesar dressing
3 green onions, sliced

**1.** Drain tomatoes, reserving ⅓ cup liquid. In large bowl, combine reserved tomato liquid with tomatoes and remaining ingredients. Season with salt and pepper to taste, if desired.

**2.** Cover and refrigerate until serving time. Garnish, if desired.

*4 servings*

**Prep Time:** 10 minutes

# EASY PINEAPPLE SLAW

1 can (15¼ ounces) DEL MONTE® Pineapple Tidbits In Its
   Own Juice, undrained
⅓ cup mayonnaise
2 tablespoons vinegar
6 cups coleslaw mix or shredded cabbage

**1.** Drain pineapple, reserving 3 tablespoons juice.

**2.** Combine reserved juice, mayonnaise and vinegar; toss with pineapple and coleslaw mix. Season with salt and pepper to taste, if desired.

*4 to 6 servings*

**Prep Time:** 5 minutes

**Caesar Shrimp Pasta Salad**

# GRILLED CHICKEN TACO SALAD

1 can (14½ ounces) DEL MONTE® Mexican Recipe Stewed
  Tomatoes
⅓ cup DEL MONTE Picante or Traditional Salsa, Hot or
  Medium
2 tablespoons vegetable oil
2 tablespoons red wine or cider vinegar
1 large head romaine lettuce, chopped (10 to 12 cups)
4 half boneless chicken breasts, grilled and cut bite size*
1 can (8 ounces) kidney beans, drained (optional)
1 cup (4 ounces) shredded sharp Cheddar cheese
3 cups broken tortilla chips

**1.** Drain tomatoes, reserving 1 tablespoon liquid. Chop tomatoes; set aside.

**2.** In small bowl, make dressing by blending reserved tomato liquid, salsa, oil and vinegar.

**3.** In large bowl, toss lettuce with tomatoes, chicken, beans and cheese. Add dressing as desired. Add chips; toss. Season with salt and pepper, if desired. Serve immediately. Garnish, if desired.      *4 main-dish servings*

**Prep Time:** 15 minutes

*Or, substitute 3 cups cubed cooked chicken.

**Tip:** To add variety to the salad, add chopped avocado, sliced green onions, olives, corn, sliced radishes and chopped cilantro, as desired.

**Grilled Chicken Taco Salad**

# LAMB SALAD WITH TOMATOES AND FETA

¾ pound boneless lamb chops (1 inch thick)
3 tablespoons olive oil
1 can (14½ ounces) DEL MONTE® Original Recipe Stewed
    Tomatoes
3 tablespoons red wine vinegar
2 to 3 tablespoons minced fresh mint *or* ½ teaspoon dried
    mint
½ medium red onion, thinly sliced
    Shredded lettuce
½ cup crumbled feta cheese

**1.** Season meat with salt and pepper, if desired.

**2.** In large skillet, heat 1 tablespoon oil over medium-high heat. Add meat; cook about 4 minutes on each side or until desired doneness. Cut meat crosswise into thin slices.

**3.** Drain tomatoes, reserving ⅓ cup liquid. Combine reserved liquid with vinegar, mint and remaining 2 tablespoons oil.

**4.** Toss meat slices, tomatoes and onion with dressing. Arrange over lettuce; top with cheese. Garnish, if desired. *4 servings*

**Prep Time:** 12 minutes
**Cook Time:** 8 minutes

**Variation:** Grill lamb over hot coals instead of pan-frying.

**Lamb Salad With Tomatoes
and Feta**

# TOMATO SCALLOPED POTATOES

1 can (14½ ounces) DEL MONTE® FRESH CUT™ Diced
    Tomatoes, undrained
1 pound red potatoes, thinly sliced
1 medium onion, chopped
½ cup whipping cream
1 cup (4 ounces) shredded Swiss cheese
3 tablespoons grated Parmesan cheese

**1.** Preheat oven to 350°F.

**2.** Drain tomatoes, reserving liquid; pour liquid into measuring cup. Add water to measure 1 cup.

**3.** In large skillet, add reserved liquid, potatoes and onion; cover. Cook 10 minutes or until tender.

**4.** Place potato mixture in 1-quart baking dish; top with tomatoes and cream. Sprinkle with cheeses.

**5.** Bake 20 minutes or until hot and bubbly. Sprinkle with chopped parsley, if desired.
*6 servings*

**Prep Time:** 8 minutes
**Cook Time:** 30 minutes

**Tomato Scalloped Potatoes**

# ARROZ MEXICANO

1 medium onion, chopped
2 cloves garlic, crushed
½ teaspoon dried oregano, crushed
1 tablespoon vegetable oil
¾ cup uncooked long-grain white rice
1 can (14½ ounces) DEL MONTE® Mexican Recipe Stewed
    Tomatoes
1 medium green bell pepper, chopped

**1.** In large skillet, cook onion, garlic and oregano in hot oil until onion is tender.

**2.** Stir in rice; cook until golden, stirring frequently.

**3.** Drain tomatoes, reserving liquid; pour liquid into measuring cup. Add water to measure 1½ cups. Stir into rice; bring to boil.

**4.** Reduce heat to medium; cover. Simmer 15 minutes or until rice is tender. Stir in tomatoes and green pepper; cook 5 minutes.

*4 to 6 servings*

**Prep Time:** 5 minutes
**Cook Time:** 27 minutes

# GOLDEN CORN PUDDING

2 tablespoons butter or margarine
3 tablespoons all-purpose flour
1 can (14¾ ounces) DEL MONTE® Cream Style Golden
    Sweet Corn
¼ cup yellow cornmeal
2 eggs, separated
1 package (3 ounces) cream cheese, softened
1 can (8¾ ounces) DEL MONTE Whole Kernel Corn,
    drained

**1.** Preheat oven to 350°F.

**2.** In medium saucepan, melt butter. Add flour and stir until smooth. Blend in cream style corn and cornmeal. Bring to a boil over medium heat, stirring constantly.

**3.** Place egg yolks in small bowl; stir in ½ cup hot mixture. Pour mixture back into saucepan. Add cream cheese and whole kernel corn.

**4.** Place egg whites in clean narrow bowl and beat until stiff peaks form. With rubber spatula, gently fold egg whites into corn mixture.

**5.** Pour mixture into 1½-quart straight-sided baking dish. Bake 30 to 35 minutes or until lightly browned. *4 to 6 servings*

**Prep Time:** 10 minutes
**Bake Time:** 35 minutes

**Tip:** Pudding can be prepared up to 3 hours ahead of serving time. Cover and refrigerate until about 30 minutes before baking.

# Pasta Perfect Meals

## MILANO SHRIMP FETTUCINE

4 ounces egg or spinach fettucine
½ pound medium shrimp, peeled and deveined
1 clove garlic, minced
1 tablespoon olive oil
1 can (14½ ounces) DEL MONTE® FRESH CUT™ Diced
    Tomatoes with Basil, Garlic & Oregano, undrained
½ cup whipping cream
¼ cup sliced green onions

**1.** Cook pasta according to package directions; drain.

**2.** Meanwhile, cook shrimp and garlic in hot oil in large skillet over medium-high heat until shrimp are pink and opaque.

**3.** Stir in tomatoes; simmer 5 minutes. Blend in cream and green onions; heat through. *(Do not boil.)* Serve over hot pasta.     *3 to 4 servings*

**Prep & Cook Time:** 20 minutes

# RAVIOLI WITH TOMATOES AND ZUCCHINI

2 packages (9 ounces *each*) fresh or frozen cheese ravioli or
  tortellini
¾ pound hot Italian sausage, crumbled
2 cans (14½ ounces *each*) DEL MONTE® FRESH CUT™
  Diced Tomatoes, undrained
1 medium zucchini, thinly sliced and quartered
1 teaspoon dried basil, crushed
½ cup ricotta cheese *or* 2 tablespoons grated Parmesan
  cheese

**1.** Cook pasta according to package directions; drain.

**2.** In large skillet or saucepan, brown sausage over medium-high heat until no longer pink; drain, reserving sausage in skillet.

**3.** Add tomatoes, zucchini and basil to skillet. Cook about 8 minutes or until zucchini is just tender-crisp, stirring occasionally. Season with pepper, if desired.

**4.** Spoon sauce over hot pasta. Top with ricotta cheese. Garnish, if desired.

*4 servings*

**Prep & Cook Time:** 20 minutes

Ravioli with Tomatoes and
Zucchini

# CHICKEN PESTO MOZZARELLA

6 to 8 ounces linguine or corkscrew pasta
4 half boneless chicken breasts, skinned
1 tablespoon olive oil
1 can (14½ ounces) DEL MONTE® FRESH CUT™ Diced
    Tomatoes with Basil, Garlic & Oregano, undrained
½ medium onion, chopped
⅓ cup sliced ripe olives
4 teaspoons pesto sauce*
¼ cup (1 ounce) shredded mozzarella cheese

**1.** Cook pasta according to package directions; drain.

**2.** Meanwhile, season chicken with salt and pepper, if desired. In large skillet, brown chicken in hot oil over medium-high heat. Add tomatoes, onion and olives; bring to boil. Cover and cook 8 minutes over medium heat.

**3.** Remove cover; cook about 8 minutes or until chicken is no longer pink in center.

**4.** Spread 1 teaspoon pesto over each chicken breast; top with cheese. Cover and cook until cheese is melted. Serve over pasta. Garnish, if desired.

*4 servings*

*Pesto sauce is available frozen or refrigerated at the supermarket.

**Prep Time:** 10 minutes
**Cook Time:** 25 minutes

**Chicken Pesto Mozzarella**

# CHICKEN PARMESAN NOODLE BAKE

1 package (12 ounces) extra-wide noodles
4 half boneless chicken breasts, skinned
¼ teaspoon rosemary, crushed
2 cans (14½ ounces *each*) DEL MONTE® Italian Recipe
    Stewed Tomatoes
½ cup (2 ounces) shredded mozzarella cheese
¼ cup (1 ounce) grated Parmesan cheese

**1.** Preheat oven to 450° F.

**2.** Cook noodles according to package directions; drain.

**3.** Meanwhile, sprinkle chicken with rosemary; season with salt and pepper, if desired. Arrange chicken in 13×9-inch baking dish. Bake, uncovered, 20 minutes or until chicken is no longer pink in center. Drain; remove chicken from dish.

**4.** Drain tomatoes, reserving liquid. In large bowl, toss reserved liquid with noodles; place in baking dish. Top with chicken and tomatoes; sprinkle with cheeses.

**5.** Bake 10 minutes or until heated through. Sprinkle with additional Parmesan cheese and garnish, if desired.                    *4 servings*

**Prep & Cook Time:** 35 minutes

Chicken Parmesan
Noodle Bake

# TOMATO PESTO LASAGNA

8 ounces lasagna noodles (2 inches wide)
1 pound crumbled sausage or ground beef
1 can (14½ ounces) DEL MONTE® FRESH CUT™ Diced
    Tomatoes with Garlic & Onion, undrained
1 can (6 ounces) DEL MONTE Tomato Paste
8 ounces ricotta cheese
1 package (4 ounces) pesto sauce*
2 cups (8 ounces) shredded mozzarella cheese

**1.** Cook noodles according to package directions; rinse, drain and separate noodles.

**2.** Meanwhile, brown meat in large skillet; drain. Stir in tomatoes, tomato paste and ¾ cup water.

**3.** In 2-quart casserole or 9-inch square baking dish, layer ⅓ meat sauce, then half *each* of noodles, ricotta cheese, pesto and mozzarella cheese; repeat layers. Top with remaining sauce. Sprinkle with grated Parmesan cheese, if desired.

**4.** Bake at 350°F, 30 minutes or until heated through.    *6 servings*

*Pesto sauce is available frozen or refrigerated at the supermarket.

**Microwave Directions:** In 9-inch square microwavable dish, assemble lasagna as directed above. Cover with vented plastic wrap; microwave on HIGH 10 minutes, rotating dish after 5 minutes.

**Prep Time:** 20 minutes
**Cook Time:** 30 minutes
**Microwave Cook Time:** 10 minutes

# TORTELLINI BAKE PARMESANO

1 package (12 ounces) fresh or frozen cheese tortellini or
    ravioli
½ pound lean ground beef
½ medium onion, finely chopped
2 cloves garlic, minced
½ teaspoon dried oregano, crushed
1 can (26 ounces) DEL MONTE® Chunky Spaghetti Sauce
    with Garlic & Herb
2 small zucchini, sliced
⅓ cup (about 1½ ounces) grated Parmesan cheese

**1.** Cook pasta according to package directions; rinse and drain.

**2.** Meanwhile, brown beef with onion, garlic and oregano in large skillet over medium-high heat; drain. Season with salt and pepper, if desired.

**3.** Add spaghetti sauce and zucchini. Cook 15 minutes or until thickened, stirring occasionally.

**4.** In oiled 2-quart microwavable dish, arrange half of pasta; top with half *each* of sauce and cheese. Repeat layers ending with cheese; cover.

**5.** Microwave on HIGH 8 to 10 minutes or until heated through, rotating dish halfway through cooking time.
*4 servings*

**Prep & Cook Time:** 35 minutes

**Helpful Hint:** For convenience, double recipe and freeze one for later use. The recipe can also be made ahead, refrigerated and heated just before serving (allow extra time in microwave if dish is chilled).

# CHEESEBURGER MACARONI

1 cup mostaccioli or elbow macaroni, uncooked
1 pound ground beef
1 medium onion, chopped
1 can (14½ ounces) DEL MONTE® Original or Italian Recipe
    Stewed Tomatoes
¼ cup DEL MONTE Tomato Ketchup
1 cup (4 ounces) shredded Cheddar cheese

**1.** Cook pasta according to package directions; drain.

**2.** In large skillet, brown meat with onion; drain. Season with salt and pepper, if desired. Stir in tomatoes, ketchup and pasta; heat through.

**3.** Top with cheese. Garnish, if desired.

*4 servings*

**Prep Time:** 8 minutes
**Cook Time:** 15 minutes

**Cheeseburger Macaroni**

# MANHATTAN TURKEY À LA KING

8 ounces wide egg noodles
1 pound boneless turkey or chicken, cut into strips
1 tablespoon vegetable oil
1 can (14½ ounces) DEL MONTE® FRESH CUT™ Diced
  Tomatoes, undrained
1 can (10¾ ounces) condensed cream of celery soup
1 medium onion, chopped
2 stalks celery, sliced
1 cup sliced mushrooms

**1.** Cook noodles according to package directions; drain.

**2.** Meanwhile, brown turkey in hot oil in large skillet over medium-high heat. Season with salt and pepper, if desired.

**3.** Add all remaining ingredients except noodles; cover. Reduce heat to medium. Cook 5 minutes. Remove cover; cook 5 minutes or until thickened, stirring occasionally.

**4.** Serve over hot noodles. Sprinkle with chopped parsley, if desired.

*6 servings*

**Prep Time:** 7 minutes
**Cook Time:** 20 minutes

**Helpful Hint:** Cook pasta ahead; rinse and drain. Cover and refrigerate. Just before serving, heat in microwave or dip into boiling water.

**Manhattan Turkey à la King**

# COUNTRY–STYLE LASAGNA

9 lasagna noodles (2 inches wide)
2 cans (14½ ounces *each*) DEL MONTE® Italian Recipe
   Stewed Tomatoes
  Milk
2 tablespoons butter or margarine
3 tablespoons all-purpose flour
1 teaspoon dried basil, crushed
1 cup diced cooked ham
2 cups (8 ounces) shredded mozzarella cheese

**1.** Cook noodles according to package directions; rinse, drain and separate noodles.

**2.** Meanwhile, drain tomatoes, reserving liquid; pour liquid into measuring cup. Add milk to measure 2 cups.

**3.** In large saucepan, melt butter; stir in flour and basil. Cook over medium heat 3 minutes, stirring constantly. Stir in reserved liquid; cook until thickened, stirring constantly. Season to taste with salt and pepper, if desired. Stir in tomatoes.

**4.** Spread thin layer of sauce on bottom of 11×7-inch or 2-quart baking dish. Top with 3 noodles and ⅓ *each* of sauce, ham and cheese; repeat layers twice, ending with cheese.

**5.** Bake uncovered at 375°F, 25 minutes. Serve with grated Parmesan cheese and garnish, if desired.

*6 servings*

**Prep Time:** 15 minutes
**Cook Time:** 25 minutes

**Country-Style Lasagna**

# GARDEN PRIMAVERA PASTA

6 ounces bow-tie pasta
1 jar (6 ounces) marinated artichoke hearts, undrained
2 cloves garlic, minced
½ teaspoon dried rosemary, crushed
1 medium green bell pepper, cut into thin strips
1 large carrot, cut into 3-inch julienne strips
1 medium zucchini, cut into 3-inch julienne strips
1 can (14½ ounces) DEL MONTE® FRESH CUT™ Diced
    Tomatoes with Garlic & Onion, undrained
12 small pitted ripe olives (optional)

**1.** Cook pasta according to package directions; drain.

**2.** Drain artichokes, reserving marinade. Combine pasta with 3 tablespoons artichoke marinade; toss to coat. Set aside. Cut artichoke hearts in half.

**3.** In large skillet, cook garlic with rosemary in 1 tablespoon artichoke marinade over medium-high heat until garlic is tender. Add all remaining ingredients except pasta and artichokes. Cook 4 to 5 minutes or until vegetables are tender-crisp and sauce is thickened.

**4.** Stir in artichoke hearts; spoon over pasta. Serve with grated Parmesan cheese, if desired.

*4 servings*

**Prep Time:** 15 minutes
**Cook Time:** 10 minutes

**Garden Primavera Pasta**

## PEANUT CHICKEN

4 half boneless chicken breasts, skinned
2 tablespoons vegetable oil
1 can (14½ ounces) DEL MONTE® Original Recipe Stewed
    Tomatoes, coarsely chopped
2 cloves garlic, minced, *or* ¼ teaspoon garlic powder
¼ teaspoon ground ginger *or* 1 teaspoon grated ginger root
⅛ to ¼ teaspoon crushed red pepper flakes
3 tablespoons chunky peanut butter

**1.** In large skillet, cook chicken in hot oil over medium-high heat about 4 minutes on each side or until chicken is no longer pink in center. Remove chicken from skillet.

**2.** Add tomatoes, garlic, ginger and red pepper flakes to skillet; cook 2 minutes. Stir in peanut butter.

**3.** Return chicken to skillet; heat through. Sprinkle with chopped cilantro and peanuts and garnish, if desired.                    *4 servings*

**Prep Time:** 4 minutes
**Cook Time:** 12 minutes

# BLACK BEAN GARNACHAS

1 can (14½ ounces) DEL MONTE® Mexican Recipe Stewed
   Tomatoes
1 can (15 ounces) black or pinto beans, drained
2 cloves garlic, minced
1 to 2 teaspoons minced jalapeño chiles (optional)
½ teaspoon ground cumin
1 cup cubed grilled chicken
4 flour tortillas
½ cup (2 ounces) shredded sharp Cheddar cheese

**1.** Drain tomatoes, reserving liquid; chop tomatoes.

**2.** In large skillet, combine tomatoes, reserved liquid, beans, garlic, jalapeño chiles and cumin. Cook over medium-high heat 5 to 7 minutes or until thickened, stirring occasionally. Stir in chicken. Season with salt and pepper, if desired.

**3.** Arrange tortillas in single layer on grill over medium coals. Spread about ¾ cup chicken mixture over each tortilla. Top with cheese.

**4.** Cook about 3 minutes or until bottoms of tortillas are browned and cheese is melted. Top with shredded lettuce, diced avocado and sliced jalapeño chiles, if desired.

*4 servings*

**Prep Time:** 5 minutes
**Cook Time:** 10 minutes

**Variation:** Prepare chicken mixture as directed above. Place a tortilla in a dry skillet over medium heat. Spread with about ¾ cup chicken mixture; top with 2 tablespoons cheese. Cover and cook about 3 minutes or until bottom of tortilla is browned and cheese is melted. Repeat with remaining tortillas.

**Black Bean Garnachas**

# SWEET AND SPICY CHICKEN STIR–FRY

1½ cups uncooked long-grain white rice
1 can (8 ounces) DEL MONTE® Pineapple Chunks In Its
    Own Juice, undrained
4 half boneless chicken breasts, skinned and cut bite-size
2 tablespoons vegetable oil
1 large green bell pepper, cut into strips
¾ cup sweet and sour sauce
⅛ to ½ teaspoon crushed red pepper flakes

**1.** Cook rice according to package directions.

**2.** Drain pineapple, reserving ⅓ cup juice.

**3.** In large skillet, stir-fry chicken in hot oil over medium-high heat until no longer pink in center. Add green pepper and reserved pineapple juice; stir-fry 2 minutes or until tender-crisp.

**4.** Add sweet and sour sauce, red pepper flakes and pineapple; stir-fry 3 minutes or until heated through.

**5.** Spoon rice onto serving plate; top with chicken mixture. Garnish, if desired.

*4 servings*

**Prep Time:** 5 minutes
**Cook Time:** 20 minutes

**Sweet and Spicy Chicken
Stir-Fry**

# HOT & SPICY BUFFALO CHICKEN WINGS

**1 can (15 ounces) DEL MONTE® Original Sloppy Joe Sauce**
**¼ cup DEL MONTE Picante or Traditional Salsa, Medium**
**1 tablespoon red wine or cider vinegar**
**20 chicken wings (about 4 pounds)**

**1.** Preheat oven to 400° F.

**2.** In small bowl, combine sloppy joe sauce, salsa and vinegar. Remove ¼ cup sauce mixture to serve with cooked chicken wings; cover and refrigerate. Set aside remaining sauce mixture.

**3.** Arrange wings in single layer in large, shallow baking pan; brush wings with sauce mixture.

**4.** On middle rack in oven, bake chicken, uncovered, 35 minutes or until chicken is no longer pink in center, turning and brushing with remaining sauce mixture after 15 minutes. Serve with reserved ¼ cup sauce. Garnish, if desired.

*4 servings*

**Prep Time:** 5 minutes
**Cook Time:** 35 minutes

**Hot & Spicy Buffalo Chicken Wings**

# FISH CAKES WITH THAI SALSA

2 cans (14½ ounces *each*) DEL MONTE® FRESH CUT™
  Diced Tomatoes with Garlic & Onion, undrained
¾ cup sliced green onions
1 tablespoon minced ginger root
¼ teaspoon crushed red pepper flakes
⅓ cup chopped cilantro
3½ cups cooked, flaked fish (1¾ to 2 pounds uncooked
  halibut, salmon or snapper)
2 eggs, beaten
½ cup Italian-seasoned dry bread crumbs
¼ cup mayonnaise
1 to 2 tablespoons butter

**1.** In medium saucepan, combine tomatoes with ½ cup green onions, ginger and red pepper flakes. Cook, uncovered, over high heat until thickened, stirring occasionally. Stir in cilantro. Cool.

**2.** In medium bowl, combine fish, eggs, crumbs, mayonnaise, remaining ¼ cup green onions and ⅓ cup tomato salsa mixture. Season with black pepper, if desired. Form into 16 patties.

**3.** Melt butter in large skillet over high heat. Reduce heat to medium-low; cook patties about 3 minutes on each side or until golden brown on both sides. Serve over salad greens, if desired. Top with salsa. Drizzle with Oriental sesame oil and garnish, if desired.          *16 (2½-inch) cakes*

**Prep & Cook Time:** 35 minutes

**Helpful Hint:** To cook fish, place in microwavable dish; cover. Microwave on HIGH 7 to 9 minutes or until fish flakes easily when tested with a fork, rotating twice; drain.

**Fish Cakes with Thai Salsa**

# FISH FRANÇOISE

1 can (14½ ounces) DEL MONTE® Original Recipe Stewed
    Tomatoes
1 tablespoon lemon juice
2 cloves garlic, minced
½ teaspoon dried tarragon, crushed
⅛ teaspoon pepper
3 tablespoons whipping cream
    Vegetable oil
1½ pounds firm white fish (such as halibut or cod)
    Lemon wedges

**1.** Preheat broiler; position rack 4 inches from heat.

**2.** In large saucepan, combine tomatoes, lemon juice, garlic, tarragon and pepper. Cook over medium-high heat about 10 minutes or until liquid has evaporated.

**3.** Stir in cream. Reduce heat to low. Cook until tomato mixture is very thick; set aside.

**4.** Brush broiler pan with oil. Arrange fish on pan; season with salt and additional pepper, if desired. Broil 3 to 4 minutes on each side or until fish flakes easily when tested with a fork.

**5.** Spread tomato mixture over top of fish. Broil 1 minute. Serve with lemon wedges.

*4 servings*

**Prep Time:** 5 minutes
**Cook Time:** 19 minutes

**Fish Françoise**

# GRILLED PRAWNS WITH SALSA VERA CRUZ

1½ cups DEL MONTE® Thick & Chunky Salsa, Mild
1 orange, peeled and chopped
¼ cup sliced green onions
¼ cup chopped cilantro or parsley
1 small clove garlic, crushed
1 pound medium shrimp, peeled and deveined

**1.** In medium bowl, combine salsa, orange, green onions, cilantro and garlic.

**2.** Thread shrimp onto skewers; season with salt and pepper, if desired.

**3.** Brush grill with oil. Cook shrimp over hot coals about 3 minutes on each side or until shrimp turn pink. Top with salsa. Serve over rice and garnish, if desired.                    *4 servings*

**Prep Time:** 25 minutes
**Cook Time:** 6 minutes

**Helpful Hint:** Thoroughly rinse shrimp in cold water before cooking.

**Grilled Prawns with
Salsa Vera Cruz**

# Best-Ever Beef, Pork & Lamb

## BEEF KABOBS WITH APRICOT GLAZE

1 can (15¼ ounce) DEL MONTE® Apricot Halves, undrained
1 tablespoon cornstarch
1 teaspoon Dijon mustard
½ teaspoon dried basil, crushed
1 pound sirloin steak, cut into 1½-inch cubes
1 small green bell pepper, cut into ¾-inch pieces
4 medium mushrooms, cut in half
4 to 8 skewers

**1.** Drain apricot syrup into small saucepan. Blend in cornstarch until dissolved. Cook over medium heat, stirring constantly, until thickened. Stir in mustard and basil. Set aside.

**2.** Thread meat, apricots, green pepper and mushrooms alternately onto skewers; brush with apricot syrup mixture. Grill kabobs over hot coals (or broil) about 5 minutes on each side or to desired doneness, brushing occasionally with additional syrup mixture. Garnish, if desired.

*4 servings*

**Prep and Cook Time:** 25 minutes

**Tip:** To prevent burning of wooden skewers, soak skewers in water for 10 minutes before assembling kabobs.

# STIR–FRY TOMATO BEEF

1 cup uncooked long-grain white rice
1 pound flank steak
1 tablespoon cornstarch
1 tablespoon soy sauce
2 cloves garlic, minced
1 teaspoon minced ginger root *or* ¼ teaspoon ground
   ginger
1 tablespoon vegetable oil
1 can (14½ ounces) DEL MONTE® Original Recipe Stewed
   Tomatoes

**1.** Cook rice according to package directions.

**2.** Meanwhile, cut meat in half lengthwise, and then cut crosswise into thin slices.

**3.** In medium bowl, combine cornstarch, soy sauce, garlic and ginger. Add meat; toss to coat.

**4.** Heat oil in large skillet over high heat. Add meat; cook, stirring constantly, until browned. Add tomatoes; cook until thickened, about 5 minutes, stirring frequently.

**5.** Serve meat mixture over hot cooked rice. Garnish, if desired.

*4 to 6 servings*

**Prep Time:** 10 minutes
**Cook Time:** 20 minutes

**Stir-Fry Tomato Beef**

# MARINATED FLANK STEAK WITH PINEAPPLE

1 can (15¼ ounces) DEL MONTE® Pineapple Slices In Its
    Own Juice, undrained
¼ cup teriyaki sauce
2 tablespoons honey
1 pound flank steak

**1.** Drain pineapple, reserving 2 tablespoons juice. Set aside pineapple for later use.

**2.** In shallow 2-quart dish, combine reserved juice, teriyaki sauce and honey; mix well. Add meat; turn to coat. Cover and refrigerate at least 30 minutes or overnight.

**3.** Remove meat from marinade, reserving marinade. Grill meat over hot coals (or broil), brushing occasionally with reserved marinade. Cook about 4 minutes on each side for rare; about 5 minutes on each side for medium; or about 6 minutes on each side for well done. During last 4 minutes of cooking, brush pineapple slices with marinade; grill until heated through.

**4.** Slice meat across grain; serve with pineapple. Garnish, if desired.

*4 servings*

**Prep & Marinate Time:** 35 minutes
**Cook Time:** 10 minutes

**Tip:** Marinade that has come into contact with raw meat must be discarded or boiled for several minutes before serving with cooked food.

**Marinated Flank Steak with Pineapple**

# TACOS PICADILLOS

¾ pound ground pork
1 medium onion, chopped
½ teaspoon ground cinnamon
½ teaspoon ground cumin
1½ cups DEL MONTE® Picante or Traditional Salsa
⅓ cup DEL MONTE Seedless Raisins
⅓ cup toasted chopped almonds
6 flour tortillas

**1.** In large skillet, brown meat with onion and spices over medium-high heat. Season to taste with salt and pepper, if desired.

**2.** Stir in salsa and raisins. Cover and cook 10 minutes. Remove cover; cook 5 minutes or until thickened, stirring occasionally.

**3.** Stir in almonds just before serving. Fill tortillas with meat mixture; roll to enclose. Serve with lettuce, cilantro and sour cream, if desired.

*6 servings*

**Prep Time:** 5 minutes
**Cook Time:** 25 minutes

**Helpful Hint:** If ground pork is not available, boneless pork may be purchased. Cut pork into 1-inch cubes before grinding in food processor.

**Tacos Picadillos**

# COUNTRY SKILLET HASH

poons butter or margarine
hops (¾ inch thick), diced
¼ teaspoon black pepper
¼ teaspoon cayenne pepper (optional)
1 medium onion, chopped
2 cloves garlic, minced
1 can (14½ ounces) DEL MONTE® Whole New Potatoes,
   drained and diced
1 can (14½ ounces) DEL MONTE® FRESH CUT™ Diced
   Tomatoes, undrained
1 medium green bell pepper, chopped
½ teaspoon thyme, crushed

**1.** In large skillet, melt butter over medium heat. Add meat; cook, stirring occasionally, until no longer pink in center. Season with black pepper and cayenne pepper, if desired.

**2.** Add onion and garlic; cook until tender. Stir in potatoes, tomatoes, green pepper and thyme. Cook 5 minutes, stirring frequently. Season with salt, if desired.

*4 servings*

**Prep Time:** 10 minutes
**Cook Time:** 15 minutes

**Tip:** The hash may be topped with a poached or fried egg.

**Country Skillet Hash**

# PORK FRIED RICE

2½ cups uncooked long-grain white rice
4 pork chops, diced
2 tablespoons vegetable oil
1 medium onion, finely chopped
1 can (14½ ounces) DEL MONTE® Peas and Carrots,
    drained
3 green onions, sliced
3 to 4 tablespoons soy sauce

**1.** Cook rice according to package directions.

**2.** In large skillet or wok, cook meat in hot oil until no longer pink in center, stirring occasionally. Add chopped onion; cook until tender.

**3.** Stir in rice, peas and carrots, green onions and soy sauce; heat through, stirring frequently. Season with pepper, if desired.      *4 servings*

**Prep & Cook Time:** 30 minutes

# LAMB WITH YOGURT MINT SAUCE

¾ pound boneless lamb or beef, cut into ¼-inch cubes
1 tablespoon olive oil
1 medium onion, cut into wedges
1 can (14½ ounces) DEL MONTE® FRESH CUT™ Diced
    Tomatoes, undrained
1 to 2 tablespoons chutney
1 teaspoon ground cumin
⅓ cup plain nonfat yogurt
1 tablespoon chopped fresh mint *or* 1 teaspoon dried mint
4 cups hot cooked pasta

**1.** In large skillet, brown meat in hot oil over medium-high heat. Stir in onion and cook 3 to 4 minutes or until tender. Add tomatoes, chutney and cumin; cook until thickened.

**2.** Combine yogurt with mint. Spoon meat mixture over hot pasta and top with yogurt mixture.

*4 servings*

**Prep Time:** 5 minutes
**Cook Time:** 12 minutes

# TABBOULI LAMB SANDWICH

1 can (14½ ounces) DEL MONTE® FRESH CUT™ Diced
    Tomatoes with Garlic & Onion, undrained
½ cup bulgur wheat, uncooked
1½ cups diced cooked lamb or beef
¾ cup diced cucumber
3 tablespoons minced fresh mint or parsley
1 tablespoon lemon juice
1 tablespoon olive oil
3 pita breads, cut into halves

**1.** Drain tomatoes, reserving liquid; pour liquid into measuring cup. Add water, if needed, to measure ¾ cup.

**2.** In small saucepan, bring reserved liquid to boil; add bulgur. Reduce heat to low; cover. Simmer 20 minutes or until bulgur is tender. Cool.

**3.** In medium bowl, combine tomatoes, meat, cucumber, mint, lemon juice and oil. Stir in cooled bulgur. Season with salt and pepper, if desired.

**4.** Spoon about ½ cup tabbouli into each pita bread half.

*6 sandwiches (½ pita each)*

**Prep & Cook Time:** 25 minutes
**Chill Time:** 30 minutes

# Delectable Desserts & More

## PINEAPPLE SWEET POTATO PIE

1 (9-inch) pastry shell, unbaked
2 cups mashed cooked sweet potatoes
⅔ cup firmly packed brown sugar
¼ cup half & half
2 tablespoons butter or margarine, melted
1 teaspoon vanilla extract
½ teaspoon cinnamon
¼ teaspoon nutmeg
¼ teaspoon salt
1 egg, beaten
1 can (15¼ ounces) DEL MONTE® Pineapple Slices In Its
   Own Juice, undrained
1 teaspoon cornstarch
1 teaspoon minced candied ginger

**1.** Prepare pastry shell; set aside.

**2.** Combine sweet potatoes, brown sugar, half & half, butter, ½ teaspoon vanilla, cinnamon, nutmeg, salt and egg; mix well. Pour into pastry shell.

*continued on page 82*

*Pineapple Sweet Potato Pie, continued*

**3.** Bake at 425°F, 25 to 30 minutes or until set in center; cool.

**4.** Drain pineapple, reserving ½ cup juice. Pour reserved juice into small saucepan. Add cornstarch; stir until dissolved. Cook, stirring constantly, until thickened and translucent. Stir in ginger and remaining ½ teaspoon vanilla.

**5.** Cut pineapple slices in half; arrange pineapple over pie. Spoon topping over pineapple. Garnish, if desired.

*8 servings*

**Prep & Cook Time:** 1 hour

# APRICOT FOSTER SUNDAE

**1 can (15¼ ounces) DEL MONTE® Unpeeled Apricot Halves
     in Heavy Syrup, undrained**
**⅓ cup firmly packed brown sugar**
**2 tablespoons butter or margarine**
**1 pint vanilla ice cream**

**1.** Drain apricot syrup into small saucepan. Bring to boil. Reduce heat to medium-low; simmer 4 minutes.

**2.** Stir in brown sugar and butter; cook until thickened, stirring constantly. Add apricots; heat through. Spoon over scoops of vanilla ice cream.

*4 servings*

**Prep & Cook Time:** 7 minutes

# PINEAPPLE MOUSSE TORTE

Chocolate Crumb Crust (recipe follows)
1 package (8 ounces) cream cheese, softened
1¼ cups sugar
½ teaspoon grated lemon peel
1 can (15¼ ounces) DEL MONTE® Crushed Pineapple In Its
    Own Juice, undrained
1 can (8 ounces) DEL MONTE Pineapple Tidbits In Its Own
    Juice, undrained
2 envelopes unflavored gelatin
2¼ cups whipping cream, whipped

**1.** Prepare crumb crust; set aside.

**2.** Blend cream cheese with sugar and lemon peel.

**3.** Drain juice from crushed pineapple and tidbits into small saucepan. Sprinkle gelatin over juice. Place over low heat and stir until gelatin is completely dissolved.

**4.** Add crushed pineapple to cream cheese mixture; stir in gelatin mixture until blended. Thoroughly fold in whipped cream.

**5.** Pour filling into crust. Chill at least 5 hours or overnight. Remove sides of pan. Top with pineapple tidbits and garnish, if desired.

*10 to 12 servings*

### CHOCOLATE CRUMB CRUST
2¼ cups chocolate wafer crumbs
½ cup butter or margarine, melted

**1.** Mix ingredients; press firmly onto bottom of 9-inch springform pan.

**Prep Time:** 20 minutes
**Chill Time:** 5 hours

# SIMPLE PEACH SORBET

**1 can (15 ounces) DEL MONTE® Peaches in Heavy Syrup**
**1 teaspoon vanilla extract**

**1.** Place unopened can of fruit in freezer; freeze until solid, approximately 24 hours (photograph 1). (Can may bulge slightly.) Submerge unopened frozen can in very hot tap water for 1 minute. Open can and pour any thawed syrup into food processor bowl.* Remove frozen fruit from can (photograph 2).

**2.** Cut fruit into 8 chunks (photograph 3). Place frozen fruit chunks in food processor; add vanilla. Process until smooth, scraping blade as needed (photograph 4). Serve immediately or spoon into freezer container and freeze until desired firmness.

*Makes 3 servings***

**Prep Time:** 8 minutes

\* Not recommended for blenders or mini food processors.
\*\* To double recipe, process in two separate batches.

**Piña Colada Sorbet:** Follow above directions using 1 can DEL MONTE Pineapple in Heavy Syrup, 2½ tablespoons well-chilled coconut milk, and if desired, ½ tablespoon rum or ½ teaspoon rum extract.

**Pear-Ginger Sorbet:** Follow above directions using 1 can DEL MONTE Pears in Heavy Syrup and ½ teaspoon minced ginger root.

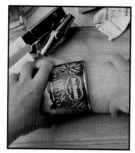

1    2    3    4

**Top to bottom: Piña Colada Sorbet, Simple Peach Sorbet, Pear-Ginger Sorbet**

# BRUSCHETTA

1 can (14½ ounces) DEL MONTE® FRESH CUT™ Diced
   Tomatoes, drained
2 tablespoons chopped fresh basil *or* ½ teaspoon dried
   basil
1 small clove garlic, finely minced
½ French bread baguette, cut into ⅜-inch-thick slices
2 tablespoons olive oil

**1.** In 1-quart bowl, combine tomatoes, basil and garlic; cover and refrigerate at least ½ hour.

**2.** Preheat broiler. Place bread slices on baking sheet; lightly brush both sides of bread with oil. Broil until lightly toasted, turning to toast both sides. Cool on wire rack.

**3.** Bring tomato mixture to room temperature. Spoon tomato mixture over bread and serve immediately. Sprinkle with additional fresh basil leaves, if desired.

*8 appetizer servings*

**Prep Time:** 15 minutes
**Cook Time:** 30 minutes

**Note:** For a fat-free version, omit olive oil. For a lower-fat variation, spray the bread with olive oil cooking spray.

**Bruschetta**

# ORCHARD FRUIT BREAD

3 cups all-purpose flour or oat flour blend
⅔ cup sugar
1 teaspoon baking soda
2 eggs, beaten
1 carton (8 ounces) lemon lowfat yogurt
⅓ cup vegetable oil
1 teaspoon grated lemon peel
1 can (15 ounces) DEL MONTE LITE® Fruit Cocktail,
    drained
½ cup chopped walnuts or pecans

**1.** Preheat oven to 350°F. Combine flour, sugar and baking soda; mix well.

**2.** Blend eggs with yogurt, oil and lemon peel. Add dry ingredients along with fruit cocktail and nuts; stir just enough to blend. Spoon into greased 9×5-inch loaf pan.

**3.** Bake 60 to 70 minutes or until wooden pick inserted into center comes out clean. Let stand in pan 10 minutes. Turn out onto wire rack; cool completely.

*1 loaf*

**Prep Time:** 15 minutes
**Cook Time:** 70 minutes

**Orchard Fruit Bread**

# PEACHY OAT BRAN MUFFINS

1½ cups oat bran
½ cup all-purpose flour
⅓ cup firmly packed brown sugar
2 teaspoons baking powder
1 teaspoon cinnamon
½ teaspoon salt
¾ cup lowfat milk
1 egg, beaten
¼ cup vegetable oil
1 can (15 ounces) DEL MONTE LITE® Yellow Cling Sliced
 Peaches, drained and chopped
⅓ cup chopped walnuts

**1.** Preheat oven to 425°F. Combine oat bran, flour, brown sugar, baking powder, cinnamon and salt; mix well.

**2.** Combine milk, egg and oil. Add to dry ingredients; stir just enough to blend. Fold in fruit and nuts.

**3.** Fill greased muffin cups with batter. Sprinkle with granulated sugar, if desired.

**4.** Bake 20 to 25 minutes or until golden brown.　　*12 medium muffins*

**Prep Time:** 10 minutes
**Cook Time:** 25 minutes

**Tip:** Muffins can be frozen and reheated in microwave or toaster oven.

**Peachy Oat Bran Muffins**

# SNAPPY COOLER

3 to 6 ounces SNAP-E-TOM® Tomato and Chile Cocktail,
   chilled
3 ounces orange juice, chilled

**1.** Combine ingredients. Serve over ice, if desired.     *1 serving*

**Prep Time:** 2 minutes

# SANGRITA

½ cup DEL MONTE® Picante or Traditional Salsa
1½ cups orange juice
  3 cups DEL MONTE Tomato Juice
    Juice of 1 medium lime

**1.** In large pitcher, mix all ingredients; chill. Serve over ice with fruit garnishes, if desired.     *6 (6-ounce) servings*

**Prep Time:** 3 minutes

# BAHAMA SLUSH

1 cup DEL MONTE® Tomato Juice, chilled
1 cup DEL MONTE Pineapple Juice, chilled
1 tablespoon lime juice
  Crushed ice

**1.** Combine juices; serve over crushed ice.     *2 (8-ounce) servings*

**Prep Time:** 2 minutes

**Left to right: Sangrita,
Snappy Cooler**

# Index